Gifted With ADD

RaeLyn Murphy
© 2011

Growing With ADD

I don't have PhD behind my name. Although I used to be in the medical field and went to college for that, I'm not an expert. So, why should you listen to me?

I have ADD which was undiagnosed and untreated. Girls with ADD most often present as "daydreamers," now medically known as "inattentive ADD." I smile about that now, because my teachers often accused me of daydreaming in school. Even as an adult, I've had people ask me 'where did you go?' or why something, such as shopping, takes so long. I get lost in what I'm doing and lose track of time. This is a common ADD symptom. I used to read in class. What the teacher was teaching was boring and often repetitive. Still, I ended up in an advanced reading and spelling class in grade school. And, while not a straight-A student, I got good grades without really studying. At least I did until I went to college. There, I tried to cram and really listen, completely changing my learning style, and it showed in my grades. I also went for nursing, although the subject left me cold. This will be an important consideration for the ADD-gifted later in the book.

My brother had ADD, but his was diagnosed and treated. I grew up "normal;" he, apparently, was diseased. He had troubles at school, had to see a psychiatrist frequently, was on medications, and had constant visits to the doctor and the principal's office.

Believe me, the principal was not his pal! It seemed like no one was. While our parents did the best they could to help him, the world must have seemed a very hostile place to him; a place where he could find no safety among adults. He ended his life in his late 20's.

I also suspect that my father, at least one uncle, and one aunt had ADD but, since it went relatively undiagnosed in those days, no one knows for sure. You see, ADD is hereditary. It's also not something you outgrow; it's a part of who you are. If you are reading this book, it is likely that you, or your spouse, already know what it's like to have this dread 'disease.' If you later recognize the symptoms in yourself and find that you, too, were undiagnosed and untreated, count yourself lucky. You have been blessed, not only in your own life, but in the better life you are now uniquely qualified to give your child. You see, ADD isn't a curse; it's the greatest blessing.

My son, Sean, has ADD. He was diagnosed at the tender age of four; an early age for such a diagnosis. All young boys are "hyperactive" and into everything. He was diagnosed mostly based on heredity. He was never put on medications however. You see, I wasn't seeking a diagnosis so that my son could repeat my brother's life. Instead, I was trying to find a way to raise a healthy child in the best way possible. Since you are reading this, I'm certain that's what you're looking for, as well.

When Sean was still very little, I would block off the stairs so he couldn't go up them. He was still crawling, barely pulling himself up, and I didn't want him falling down the stairs. But, he'd somehow figured a way to get over the gate. As soon as he got over it, he'd start laughing hysterically because he'd gotten away with it. While this wasn't my first sign that Sean had ADD, it was an inkling into just how smart he was. Even at the age of one and a half, people were telling me he was "all boy." I was naive enough to think this was a compliment. At a doctor's appointment around the age of two, his pediatrician made the same statement, noting how Sean was trying to take apart the office lamp. Sean challenged the child care center when he figured out how to open up the door. Holding the door for all of his "classmates" he said 'Come on, we're free! Let's Go!' He was not yet three years old.

By the time he was three or four, no doors could keep him. The front door needed a deadbolt with a key, because he could open a regular deadbolt. Child proof door locks didn't hold him; he had it open before I'd even had the chance to put away the installation tools. An old-fashioned spring-loaded hook and eye far above his head was the only thing that could keep him. He craved attention and had no emotional control. Temper tantrums sounded like he was being abused. As a parent, it was emotional torture. Not only could I not control my child, but his behavior was humiliating. I was very aware of how his behavior and my lack of ability to adequately discipline him reflected on me as a parent.

I called a parenting hotline. In those days, around 1989, corporal punishment was extremely taboo. Spankings were considered child abuse; they were teaching this in school. The parenting hotline told me to put him in time out. I tried. I would put Sean in time out, he'd get up. I'd firmly put him back in time out; he'd get up. By the end of five or ten minutes of this I wanted to spank him for not staying in time out and neither of us could remember what he'd done to deserve the time out! The parenting hotline would say to ignore his tantrums while in time out. He had to sit quietly before it could start. Right! Like that ever happened...NOT!

I tried locking him in his room, which is something that bothered even me. He'd kick the door and scream until I let him out. Then, he started peeing on the carpet. Clearly, this was not the solution.

I called the local children's hospital. Actually, that turned out to be the best thing I could have done. They, at least, provided me with some disciplinary actions that worked. I'm not sure where I actually got the information now. It's not like you can just randomly call a hospital and get answers. I believe I called Social Services. Right now, hospital social workers are having a fit that I've dared to write that in a book to people reaching for help, but hospital social workers are, hands down, *the* most connected people. More than the over-worked county social worker, hospital social workers know about programs that few people are remotely aware of. These under-appreciated groups of people are truly miracle workers, but I digress.

I was taught to use 1-2-3 Magic and an acronym which I no longer remember. I believe it was FIRE, remembering mostly that it ended with escape, which was some of the best advice on Earth.

Things settled down. Also, my husband became a house father and I went to work third shift. This helped to completely change the dynamic that had been escalating with Sean's behavior and its continual assault on the family senses. If you're thinking that ADD doesn't sound like much of a gift yet, you're right. It didn't feel like much of one at this point.

Since he was born in late fall, Sean didn't start school until he was almost six. He couldn't wait to start school and wanted to make friends. The ADD-gifted are very social people. Sean wanted to experience everything all at once. He wanted to know everything, to do everything. He'd been that way since he was born. And still, everyone was telling me he was "all boy." His kindergarten teacher was impressed with his vocabulary and he thrived in kindergarten. I wasn't surprised; his teacher was as energetic as he was. They never stayed on one subject for long; I doubt Sean had the chance to be bored. This would become even more evident when my daughter attended kindergarten: she needed to finish things before moving on to the next thing and that didn't happen in this teacher's class.

By first grade, Sean's ADD had become quite evident. He couldn't sit in class and started causing trouble on the playground. It wasn't the kind of trouble that one would really consider "trouble" as much as that his desire to do everything met with resistance, especially from the older children. Also, he refused to come in from recess. His teacher was aware of his diagnosis. It was all over his school records, as if it were a health problem because, frankly, we thought it was. Bless her heart; she tried very hard to work with Sean. He told me, at the age of seven, and in front of a teacher he actually really liked, "She asks the same question over and over, just in different ways. We've got it already." This is yet another symptom of ADD; they're faster thinkers than their "normal" classmates and they tend to pick things up more quickly. His teacher did try to take advantage of his quick-thinking mind. She encouraged Sean to help students around him so that they could keep up. It was a good thought, although Sean never has had much in the way of tolerance for people who "don't get it."

Nevertheless, about half way through the school year, we brought him home to home-school after the principal called me and said "I think your son has ADD." My response was "REALLY?! What was your first clue?" Honestly, that's what I said. He thoroughly annoyed me. He wanted Sean on medication; I pulled him out of school. We had been looking into home-schooling as an option for two years already.

Sean's struggle to find his way would see him in and out of school at various times due to the ignorance of teaching staff and the inability of public schools to properly teach, or provide for, the ADD-gifted. He devoured books and information. Teaching him was a breeze. He just needed more social interaction than Boy Scouts, Awanas, summer sports, and the local home-schooling group could provide.

Seventh grade was a nightmare. By high school, I didn't feel we were adequately able to provide a proper education. Sean participated in three sports and maintained honor roll grades without a single visit to the principal's office throughout his freshman and sophomore year. He started attending the local tech college at 16 and graduated at a time when the majority of his classmates were walking across the high school stage.

Gifted With ADD © 2011 RaeLyn Murphy

This is not the end of Sean's story, of course. He's 25 now and very successful. I'm extremely proud of him. This is, however, the beginning of the solution. This is also not a book about home-schooling, but if you think that you could not spend that much time with your child, I'd implore you to think again. I learned so much about my son and the amazing, magnificent person that he is from spending that much time with him. He picks things up at an utterly amazing speed and retains it. His hunger for knowledge is inspiring. He's compassionate and social, charming and playful. He's also very ambitious and industrious. He likes to work with his hands and is extremely creative, something which shows as much in his music as it does in his ability to problem-solve. Even at four, he could add the dice in Monopoly® or Yahtzee® almost before they'd finished landing. The man is just brilliant; just another "symptom" of the ADD-gifted. Once you stop battling against the "disease," your child's true spirit shines through.

Hopefully, you can see some of these amazing qualities in your child already. If you are among the blessed who were mistreated as a child, I hope you can find these qualities in yourself. I wasn't an awesome parent; *we* weren't awesome parents. None of our children would accuse us of that. We did the best we could and I couldn't be more proud of the man Sean has become or more pleased with the relationship we have. Still, for as many trials as we had throughout his childhood, I can honestly say that I miss the boy he was. If nothing else, that's what I hope this book accomplishes: that not only will you learn to deal with ADD effectively, but that you will come to appreciate and enjoy the exuberant,

Gifted With ADD © 2011 RaeLyn Murphy

passionate, and amazing child you have the privilege to watch grow up.

Author's Note: For ease of reading, your child will be referred to in the generic "he," not because everyone with ADD is male, but because the majority of children who drive their parents to seek help for ADD are male. And it's just easier.

Table Of Contents

Growing With ADD   2
Life As A Disease   10
    ADD/ADHD Diagnosis   16
        School
        Medical/Psychological
        Medications
        Ongoing Treatment
    Life As A Disease or Disability   27
The Gift of ADD   30
        He's A Creative Thinker
        He's Curious
        He Can Hyper-Focus
        He Sees Links That Others Miss
        He Has An Incredible Ability To Multi-Task
        He Is Enthusiastic And Energetic
        He's a Dreamer And More Interested in Creative Pursuits
Positive Parenting   35
    Working With (ADD) Nature   37
        Try to have a family routine.
        Give him time.
        Transition to bedtime.
        Pick your battles.
        Give him choices, not commands.
        Let him save face.
        Play to his problem-solving ability.
        Listen and try to see his point of view.
        Recognize success.

Gifted With ADD © 2011 RaeLyn Murphy

- Reward early, reward often, and keep it positive.
- Make things easy on yourself.
- Have a Special Time.
- Take care of you.

Schools   46
- Public School Success   49
  - The Teacher Is NOT The Enemy
  - Tips For School Success At Home
- Alternatives to School   56
  - Home-Schooling
  - Unschooling
  - Montessori Schools
  - Democratic/Sudbury Schools
  - Waldorf Education
  - Coalition of Essential Schools
  - College Instead of High School
  - 'How Are We Going To Pay For That?'
  - Conclusion

Adults with ADD   80
Be Like Water   83

Life as a Disease

Take a moment to look at the disease through the eyes of your child. If you grew up with ADD, your perspective right now is seen through the lens of someone with a "disease" that feels "normal" to you. You probably don't really feel handicapped or abnormal; it's all you've ever known. What differs from child to child is how others experience that child and how they will, therefore, experience others. If, however, you have been taught that you have shortcomings such as the inability to organize, focus, and remember things, you might be more aware of "life as a disease."

ADD is hereditary. As such, it's not something you can reasonably expect your child to grow out of. If he were born with green eyes, you wouldn't expect them to turn brown. Likewise, if your child were born deaf, you would not expect him to suddenly begin to hear. When your child was born, he may have seemed more alert than other babies, or than you expected. Perhaps he seemed to pick up on things easier. Children, especially newborns, are all so different, however. It is unlikely that, as an infant, there was a very noticeable difference that could be directly tied to ADD. And so, you happily began to raise a beautiful child.

By the age of three or four, children begin to develop minds of their own. They learn, and test, the word "no." They begin to get into everything and the ADD child begins to demonstrate an almost annoying thirst for knowledge and a need to try everything, including your patience! As a parent, we reasonably expect to be able to set limits and have them respected, as well as a three or four year old can respect them. They are tactual and want to touch everything. They seek attention from you constantly and their energy levels may be so high that you feel as if you cannot go to the bathroom without them getting into trouble. It's impossible to make dinner, forget talking on the phone, visiting with friends is a nightmare. No matter who wears the pants in the family, the child with ADD is calling all the shots.

At this point, if not a bit earlier, the power struggles begin in earnest. The more you try to limit his behavior, the more he acts up. He won't sit down to eat. He throws temper tantrums when you try to limit his behavior. You have to tell him something four times before he listens, if he listens at all. With four year old preschool becoming more prevalent, parents begin to look at their child's behavior critically a bit younger because we know they will have to fit into a peer environment, which further increases parent-child tension.

Now look at it from his point of view. He has so much energy within his body that he just has to go, but he has begun to be told that his behavior is unacceptable. He physically cannot control the amount of energy in his body and finds he can't sit for very long. Television may not hold his interest. He can't stay at the table to eat. It is difficult to sit in the car for long periods of time.

His mind is racing from topic to topic so that he is interested in building blocks one moment and onto cars the next. On the other hand, there are times when he focuses on something so intently that time disappears and he honestly doesn't hear you. This will often happen when he's problem-solving or creating/building something. It can also happen when he is reading, which an ADD child does have the ability to do.

His actions, at times, appear impulsive, but he doesn't feel impulsive at all. Details are the domain of careful thought, which is a slow process. Children with ADD are fast-thinkers; they don't "think things through" because they don't pay attention to details. They don't remember things because they're only half-listening. They're so easily distracted, even with their own thoughts, that they forget to pay attention to the things they are supposed to be grabbing from their locker, so they show up to class "unprepared" and they go home without their homework.

Despite being quick thinkers, ADD children don't do well with rapid or frequent changes. They need time to assimilate. Over-stimulation feels like a buildup of energy in the body, as if dammed behind a wall. If uninterrupted, it builds up like a volcano within him until it explodes into an emotional response that he has little or no control over. A quiet environment, on the other hand, is boring. In his search for stimulation, he creates excitement or chaos.

All of this feels perfectly normal to the ADD child. It's always felt this way; he was born this way. So, consider how the limits feel. As a parent, sitting at the dinner table is a reasonable expectation, but he can't physically do it. He wants to please you. He wants to do the things you want him to do. So, he'll try. But, he'll wriggle in his seat, kick the legs of the table, lean his chair back on its legs, and play with his food. He's there, but it's difficult for him. This same dynamic applies to time out. You're expecting a child who can't sit still or handle periods of silence to be quiet and sit still, as a punishment.

He is consistently admonished for getting into things, but to him it's just a natural state of curiosity. He's a hands-on learner. He can't wait his turn; his mind is going a hundred miles an hour and, even at the age of four, he's trying to get people to listen to him because he thinks he knows what's up. What happens when everything that feels natural is wrong? How does a four year old process the first signs of rejection or the first indications that something about him is just "not right?"

By the time school starts, it is almost a relief to have him gone for a block of time and you feel guilty for thinking that. You also wonder how he's going to do at school when he won't behave at home. Perhaps you've even had trouble finding a baby-sitter who could watch him because his behavior is so time-intensive. Your life is in chaos because of emotional stress and the inability to find a moment to yourself. If you have other children, you may worry that they play second fiddle to the needs of the one with the problems. Indeed, it is sometimes easier to give in to the ADD child just to keep the peace. On the flip-side, you may work extremely hard to keep him under control. Either way, his problems quickly become the main focus of everyone.

ADD is most often diagnosed once the child starts school. Here, peer pressure is used as early as kindergarten and first grade to get children to conform.

If the students are lining up, all students are expected to line up. When it is time to clean up and move onto something else, it is expected of the entire class that they do so. Likewise, if all of the students are sitting for story time, it is not acceptable for one child to start playing with the building blocks.

If he's adequately stimulated, your child may not show many signs of problems until he is expected to sit in his desk and pay attention in first grade. At this point, a diagnosis may be sought and you are faced with treatment options as well as parenting techniques.

ADD/ADHD Diagnosis

School
If your child is struggling academically, the school may offer a multi-disciplinary team evaluation (MDE). In most states, this cannot be conducted without your permission. However, in some states, it can be conducted if you are notified and fail to respond. Check with your local school district's Special Education department for rules and procedures in your area.

Parents are part of the MDE team, as are counselors, teachers, and administrators. The purpose of the evaluation is to identify the areas that are causing the student to struggle and to create a working plan to help the child get the best education possible. To do this, multiple tests are given. An IQ test cannot be the only test given because one test alone will be inadequate to determine the cause of problems in the classroom.

There are a few guidelines that must be followed, however:
- The tests must be given in the student's first language.
- The tests must accurately assess a problem other than inadequate language skills.
- The tests cannot be cultural, racial, or discriminatory in any way.

Once the tests are completed, the team will get together to discuss the best course of action and an individualized education plan (IEP) should be agreed upon and instituted. Re-evaluation will usually take place within 90 days to identify what is working and what still needs to change. From there, re-evaluation takes place periodically, usually once per school year, as needed.

Medical/Psychological

Medical diagnosis may vary by doctor and region. There should first be a thorough parent interview. This will probably take at least 45 minutes to an hour, but it may be longer or shorter, depending on the history and the doctor. In this interview, the therapist will want to obtain a detailed history. This will include a health history, as well as a history of your child's behavior. They will want to find out if there have been health problems such as
- birth injury
- problems during the pregnancy
- history of drug/alcohol abuse during pregnancy
- frequent ear infections
- frequent illnesses

- a history of head injury, accidents, fevers, seizures, etc.
- a family history of ADD/ADHD, Tourettes, Obsessive-Compulsive Disorder, Schizophrenia, Alcoholism, depression, and learning disabilities.

Developmentally, they will want to know
- When did your child learn to roll over, walk, potty train, etc.?
- Were there were any problems with speech?
- Have there been any developmental concerns?

There are a number of things your medical care giver is trying to evaluate your child for. ADD/ADHD is not necessarily the most obvious diagnosis. Seizures, for instance, may present as hyperactivity and will cause inattentiveness. Head injuries may also present in this way. There may also have been an inciting event. Perhaps your child is reacting to marital problems, a new move, a new school, a death in the family or the loss of a friend. He might be suffering from anxiety or depression. There may also be visual or auditory difficulties. Different disorders require different treatments, so it is important to evaluate carefully.

You may be given the Ned Owens or Keith Connors rating scales to fill out. See the following pages for a copy of the Ned Owens evaluation. An example of the Connors Test can be found online at http://www.noranclinic.com/downloads/connors_parents.pdf . Teachers may also be given similar forms to return to your child's therapist or practitioner.

Finally, there should be an extensive interview with your child. During this time, the therapist or psychologist is both evaluating your child's behavior as well as assessing what is going on in your child's world from the child's point of view. There may be something going on that you, as parents, are unaware of. This is the opportune time to determine if there is something other than a disease process that is causing your child to act out.

A.D.D BEHAVIOR RATING SCALES
By Ned Owens M.Ed.
Betty White Owens

Name_____DOB__
_____Age_____ Grade_____
Date_____

Rate EVERY statement by placing the appropriate number which most fits the student's behavior in the box opposite the statement.

1. You have not noticed this behavior before.
2. You have noticed this behavior to a slight degree.
3. You have noticed this behavior to a considerable degree.
4. You have noticed this behavior to a large degree.
5. You have noticed this behavior to a very large degree.

1. Fails to complete assigned tasks……………………………………..………………………..

2. Often acts before thinking………………………………..……………………………..

3. Runs or climbs a great deal……………………………………………………..……………..

4. Gets mad easily………………………………………………………..

Gifted With ADD © 2011 RaeLyn Murphy

5. Is a poor reader..

6. Doesn't seem to listen or pay attention..

7. Shifts excessively from one activity to another..

8. Has difficulty staying seated..

9. Shows anger when told to do something..

10. Is a poor speller..

11. Poor concentration on difficult tasks..

12. Can't seem to organize school work..

13. Has difficulty sitting still: fidgets..

14. Is easily frustrated..

15. Does not follow verbal directions..

16. Doesn't stick to just one play activity (changes a lot)..

17. Needs a lot of supervision..

18. Moves excessively during sleep or "rocks" in daytime..

19. Lose temper easily..

20. Handwriting is poor (may vary day to day)..

21. Is distracted easily..

22. Interrupts or speaks out of turn..

23. On the go much of the time..

24. Can't take teasing..

25. Has difficulty in completing homework..

26. Is afraid of many things..

27. Doesn't trust himself or "downs" himself..

Gifted With ADD © 2011 RaeLyn Murphy

28. Delights in others failures or getting in trouble..

29. Exhibits stubbornness..

30. Has "I don't care" attitude..

31. Worries about many things..

32. Seems satisfied with poor school work..

33. Pushes or shoves classmates..

34. Resists being disciplined..

35. Is untruthful and may cheat at games..

36. Is easily embarrassed...

37. Doesn't compete with others..

38. Tries to boss other children..

39. Blames others for his mistakes or behavior...

Gifted With ADD © 2011 RaeLyn Murphy

40. Makes promises but doesn't keep them..

41. Appears nervous...

42. Is easily frustrated and gives up quickly..

43. Makes derogatory remarks about others...

44. Must have his own way..

45. Steals...

46. Appears tense...

47. Has little confidence..

48. Plays tricks on others or teases...

49. Will not take suggestions...

50. Does not respect authority...

Gifted With ADD © 2011 RaeLyn Murphy

Rated by
_____

___
Relationship to Child
_____

___

In addition to the ratings scales, several tests may be performed. The WISC-R (Wechsler Intelligence Scale for Children-Revised) is an IQ test. The WRAT (Wide Range Achievement Test) measures skills in math, reading, and spelling. There are two levels to this test based on age groups. The Bender Visual Motor Gestalt Test is used to assess visual-motor skills and visual perception. The Test of Variables of Attention (T.O.V.A. ®) is a game-like computer test that monitors reaction times and how your child processes visual and auditory information.

Medications

While it is the purpose of this book to arm you with enough information to make informed decisions, it is not the purpose of this book to offer skewed information. It is not, however, outside of the scope of this book to point out that many of them medications are stimulants and contain the word amphetamine (Speed). You will do what is best for your family; just make informed decisions.

You are encouraged to learn as much as possible about medications before your doctor offers them and before you start giving them to your child. Unbiased medication information, including warnings and side effects can be found at http://www.ncbi.nlm.nih.gov/pubmedhealth/ and http://www.fda.gov/Drugs/DrugSafety/ucm085729.htm .

Medications for children with ADD/ADHD include:
- Ritalin (Methylphenidate)
- Wellbutrin (Bupropion)
- Dexedrine (Dextroamphetamine)
- Metadate CD (Methylphenidate)~Extended Release
- Daytrana (Methylphenidate Transdermal) ~It's a patch.
- Adderall (Dextroamphetamine and Amphetamine)
- Strattera (Atomoxetine)
- Focalin (Dexmethylphenidate)
- Vyvanse (Lisdexamfetamine)

Ongoing Treatment

As a hereditary disease, ADD is not out-grown. Treatment, therefore, will be an ongoing process. Therapies for your child and family may include medical visits for medication and evaluation, behavioral psychiatry, and cognitive-behavioral therapy.

Cognitive-behavioral therapy allows the child to talk about upsetting thoughts and feelings, learn alternative ways to handle emotions, identify and build on their strengths, explore alternatives to self-defeating behaviors, cope with daily problems, and control their attention and aggression. When it is used as part of family therapy, parents may learn better ways to handle disruptive behaviors and gain insight into problems that are cropping up in their child's daily life.

Behavioral therapy focuses more on ways to deal with immediate issues. It tackles thinking and coping patterns directly, without trying to understand their origins. Its purpose is to change behavior and to deal with frustrations and anger issues as they occur.

Life As A Disease or Disability

Everyone needs to make decisions for their child that are best for the child. It is not for me or for anyone else, medical or otherwise, to decide what is best for your child. As parents, all you can do is arm yourself with the most information you can find and then decide what will be best for your family and for your son or daughter.

If you decide to go the medical route, you will still have options: what medications, how much care, and what kinds of treatments. As you go through this process, check yourself frequently to make sure your decisions still resonate with your feelings.

Whether or not you choose medication and treatment, you will have to deal with the symptoms into adulthood and your child still needs to learn to live within the confines of his "disease" to step into mainstream society. You will need to be his advocate throughout his development. Labels are difficult to remove and add a greater stigma to someone who is already trying to find their way. With ADD there can be a tendency to rely on the ADD label, not only for parents, but for teachers, bus drivers, principals, caregivers, family and friends.

For parents and family, once your child is diagnosed with an "incurable disease," no matter what the disease, there is a strong tendency for life to center on dealing with the disease (dis-ease). One message becomes the broken record of life in your household: 'there's something wrong with my child.' Your child gets that message loud and clear, but not just from you.

At school, teachers, principals, counselors, bus drivers and playground supervisors all develop a vested interest in your child's care. You will start to hear 'How do you think that medication is working out for him?' 'Are you trying something new? He seems to be acting up more lately.' 'How are things going at home?' There is always that feel of genuine concern and an interest to help, but the end result is that your child knows that everyone is talking about him and that's not a good thing. He may also be pulled from class for counseling, evaluation, special education subjects, and meetings. On a bad day, a teacher will say something about his ADD in front of the whole class or make or make it known that he needs his medication. Schools also regulate medications, so that any dosages he receives at school are also given that small but extra significance.

The family schedule now has to include therapy sessions, doctor visits, extra time at the school for meetings, and trips to the pharmacy (which may also strain the family budget). Most likely, when you went to seek a diagnosis, you wanted to make your child's life easier; you wanted to make things easier on the family. So, why has everything suddenly gotten so much harder?

Gifted With ADD © 2011 RaeLyn Murphy

It's kind of like fighting nature. Dying your raven black hair blonde is a lot of work and upkeep, but it can be done. It's also a fairly expensive process if you want to do it in a healthy manner. If you take a break from fighting nature, your natural hair color begins to show through and you must choose to continue the fight or let nature take over.

Your child's natural state is one of high energy (if he has ADHD), minimal focus, and general inattentiveness. You can try to fight this natural state, as if it's a disease, and hope for a positive outcome, but it will always be an uphill battle.

The Gift of ADD

Your ADD-gifted child can't sit in a desk, face forward and listen to a teacher drone on about some boring subject he may not ever apply to his life anyway. So what? OK, that's a dramatic over-simplification and, if it weren't for some form of education, none of us could read, write, or do the math that our jobs require. We wouldn't have historians, librarians, doctors, lawyers, or the Internet.

However, the over-simplification has a point. General education public schools aren't trying to teach children like yours. They cater to kids who can sit still, face forward and listen to boring subjects. The fact of the matter is that your child isn't going to have to do a job in his life that requires him to do that. In fact, name a job which requires that daily? You may be able to, but your child isn't going to do that job anyway. He's not cut out to be a retail employee or to sit behind a desk all day, but that doesn't mean he won't have meaningful work or fit into society, so why try to fit your square peg into this particular round hole anyway? Stop trying to groom your quick, intelligent child for a mindless or mediocre job/life. Save yourself, and your child, the headache by playing to his strengths instead of focusing on his weaknesses. Your ADD-gifted child has several strengths to play to.

He's A Creative Thinker

People with ADD have a stream of consciousness running through their heads at all times. In fact, it's very difficult to slow that process down. For this reason, ideas flow freely. Remember that the ADD-gifted don't pay attention to details because that would require focus, which is something they have difficulty with. The same symptom that causes your child to appear impulsive prevents him from negating an idea before it comes to light. He doesn't stop at one right answer, nor does he immediately censor his ideas the way his "rapid thought-impaired" peers do. Usually, there are many solutions to a problem; the ADD-gifted are just more aware of this.

He's Curious

Contrary to popular belief, children with ADD *can* learn. They have a remarkable hunger for information and will devour information that is presented in the right ways. This is something you will learn and hear often: "*IF* he's interested." However, when he's interested and engaged, I dare you to try to stop the learning process. You won't want to; it's inspiring to watch. But, if you tried, you'd likely fail. The ADD-gifted are extremely adept at finding information and persistent about taking it all in at once. Some might find this a problem; certainly, it's a problem in a normal classroom. Math time is math time and the class is working on fractions, but your child wants to experiment with the beakers and chemicals in science class instead. Either that, or it comes time to put the math books away and move on, but he's still interested in learning more about advanced fractions. He doesn't learn on a classroom schedule, which goes at much too slow a pace for his fast-thinking brain anyway.

Gifted With ADD © 2011 RaeLyn Murphy

He Can Hyper-Focus

Distractibility is a mark of boredom, for the most part. When the ADD-gifted are engaged, they can hyper-focus. When your child does this, some people will tell you he doesn't have ADD/ADHD. How can he? He's sitting still and he's not daydreaming. In fact, he's so focused that you can't get his attention. You will notice this especially if he is trying to work out a puzzle, playing a game, reading a book, exploring, or creating. As long as the task is interesting, the ability to hyper-focus grants an edge in the amount of work the ADD-gifted can accomplish when compared to those who are ADD-deficient.

He Sees Links That Others Miss

This is part of that creative thinking because it uses that same stream of consciousness. "I like ice cream....We used to make ice cream at Bark Lake...A lake made of bark, that's funny...We used to get chocolate bark at the candy store...We should make blue moon ice cream with chocolate chunks in it and call it Bark Lake." That makes perfect sense to the ADD-gifted, but many would never make the jump from ice cream to a new "Bark Lake" flavor. Keep in mind, also, that there are no pauses in that train of thought for the ADD-gifted. It looks more like this: I like ice cream we used to make ice cream at Bark Lake a lake made of bark, that's funny we used to get chocolate bark at the candy store we should make blue moon ice cream with chocolate chunks in it and call it Bark Lake." In creative environments, this is a very useful trait.

He Has An Incredible Ability To Multi-Task

In the early years, especially during elementary school years, the uses for this ability may not be as evident.

Instead, it will present as a child who only spends ten minutes on math before getting out the spelling book. He bores of that easily and moves onto something else, never really able to focus on the task at hand. These are the children who are sent to the garage for a shovel and spend a half hour re-arranging Dad's tools. They become adults who go to the kitchen to make a cup of coffee and end up emptying the dishwasher, thawing out meat, and talking on the phone, completely forgetting the coffee until it is cold in the cup. As a working adult, however, these are the people who can switch between three software programs, write while talking on the phone and watching TV on the second screen of their PC. If you can help your child navigate childhood successfully with this skill intact, it will serve him well in his future career.

He Is Enthusiastic And Energetic

The ADD-gifted have an incredible ability to stay on a project until it is finished, out-distancing other teams by miles, as long as the project holds his interest. As a child, this may not be immediately obvious because family routines break up the day naturally. As a career-oriented adult, he will have an advantage over those who need stimulants just to make it through the day. His enthusiasm and passion for the project is contagious and will quickly infect the team, adding more fuel to the project's development speed.

He's a Dreamer And More Interested in Creative Pursuits

So are Will Smith, Justin Timberlake, Michael Phelps, Jim Carrey, Ty Pennington, Sir Richard Branson, Howie Mandel, Terry Bradshaw, Paul Orfalea (Founder of Kinko's), Pet Rose, Michelle Rodriguez, David

Neeleman (Founder of JetBlue Airways), Bruce Jenner, and many more. Albert Einstein is said to have had ADD; Walt Disney, as well. This has not prevented any of them from becoming some of our most gifted comedians, Olympians, writers, politicians, athletes, actors/actresses, inventors, and entrepreneurs. The activities these well-known figures took part in helped them focus the symptoms of ADD/ADHD; the "syndrome" helped them attain the successes they have today.

Diagnosis is important because ADD/ADHD is very real. However, instead of thinking in terms of how to "fix" your child, use the diagnosis to learn how to build the systems he needs to succeed. Become an advocate for your child and surround yourself with people who are interested in helping him grow rather than in stifling his innate abilities. He has a tremendous gift which only becomes a curse when the message is that he needs "fixing" because he was born "broken." Will there be difficult times? Of course there will. ADD children are strong-willed, they can be stubborn, and they don't fit into the standard molds. They throw temper tantrums in the store, kick the back of your seat while you are driving and can be difficult to keep in a car seat. Like any child, when you are on his side, he will bring you great joy and make you proud. He will also get on your last nerve almost daily. At that point, you won't believe that ADD is a gift. His teachers won't tell you it's a gift. You have to be the vision holder and make sure it remains one.

Gifted With ADD © 2011 RaeLyn Murphy

Positive Parenting

Positive Parenting is a very cliché' term at the moment. It's the politically correct way of saying "Don't spank." "Don't hit or yell." "Don't argue with your child." "Don't enter into power struggles with your children." When you think about it, though, the best thing you can do for your own sanity and for your relationship with your children is arm yourself with a positive outlook from the beginning.

One barrier to positive parenting is the concept of family hierarchy and discipline. If you and your parenting partner feel that you need to be in charge and your children must "hop to," you are destined for power struggles with your strong-willed ADD child. Do yourself a favor and consider the reasons that you think you must "discipline" your children and how well a "boss" works in a cooperative environment vs. a "team leader." In your own career, have you done better with a boss who was part of the team or one who set themselves above the team, seeming as if they had no idea of what went on in the "real world" of your job. Children aren't small adults, but they are perceptive *people*. They want respect from their superiors, especially the ones who are in their inner circle.

When Sean was in seventh grade, his multidisciplinary team at school decided that he didn't have ADD; he had ODD (Oppositional-Defiant Disorder). We'll skip right past the fact that a bunch of teachers and counselors felt qualified to diagnose my son and onto the fact that Sean was deeply proud of this. "I AM defiant and oppositional" he'd say. When you enter into an argument with your child and you end up frustrated, he wins. He also learns which buttons to push and he will push them. Don't get hung up on controlling your children. The things that mortify you today are things you will laugh at later; you may even find yourself missing the child he was when he has grown. That's hard to believe now, but it happens. ADD children tend to have a wonderful sense of humor and a charming way about them; you'll miss his exuberance. Try to maintain your sense of humor.

The reason we "discipline" our children is because we are trying to teach them to be upstanding members of society and productive adults. We fear that, if they don't do well in school, they will be failures as adults. Look at that list of successful ADD celebrities again. Many of them struggled in school. Relax a little. You're actually trying to teach your children how to act; negative reinforcement, or punishment, rarely serves this purpose. I'm not saying you should compromise or give into the tyrant, allowing your children to run roughshod over you, the parents. Instead, treat them as if you expect them to be reasonable and as if you respect that they will make mistakes because they are still learning. This is also not to say that they won't do naughty things on purpose. They will. It's not personal. If you arm yourself with a plan, you can deal with these moments without frying your own nerves. You'll slip up, too. Forgive yourself. It happens. A Lot.

Gifted With ADD © 2011 RaeLyn Murphy

Working With (ADD) Nature

Try to have a family routine.
It doesn't have to be, and shouldn't be, a strict routine. It should be fluid. If you are a perfectionist who needs constant order, you may struggle with this. Again, try to let go a little. Make things as easy on yourself as possible. Much of living with a child with ADD/ADHD is actually about making things easier on yourself. Children with structure, expectations, and chores feel secure and loved, even when they are calling you "mean." However, if the structure is too rigid or meeting the expectations becomes a battle, you are only setting yourself up for power struggles.

Give him time.
When you are going to switch gears, give your child a heads up. Even if it is part of the regular routine, you'll find your child is more cooperative when he gets forewarning. Keep age in mind. Ten minutes doesn't mean as much to a four year old as "when this show is over" does. Give him landmarks. "When the next commercial break comes on, you need to get your shoes on so we can go to the store." "In 15 minutes, it will be reading time." Be as specific as you can be. If you say "We can go when I finish with the laundry," for instance, he probably has no idea how long the laundry will take you. If you are the parent with ADD, you might also tend to start laundry and do something else, meaning you won't stick strictly to that deadline.

Transition to bedtime.
Turn off the lights for at least one hour before bedtime. Settle into a more quiet routine. Allow each child to pick

one story or one book to read before bed. You have to slow down the engine in your child's body if you want him to go to bed.

Pick your battles.
Decide what you can live with. In school, and at home, you will find it essential, at some point, to pick your battles. If he won't do one chore today, but he did his other two, brushed his teeth and did his homework, praise him for the good job on everything else and let the chore go. If he's doing his homework, but sitting sideways in his chair with his homework on his lap, be happy he's doing his homework and let it go. You are raising him to be independent; try to value that independence.

Give him choices, not commands.
Let him make some decisions for himself. This is an excellent way to direct him to make decisions that are acceptable to you while allowing him to feel empowered. If you don't want him wearing shorts to school, you might give him a choice between the jeans and the khaki pants. Ask him if he'd rather wear the red shirt or the blue shirt leaving out the shirt he might prefer to wear because it's torn, in the wash today, or inappropriate in some other way. Ask him if he'd like to play for 15 minutes before starting homework or get right in on the homework. Wherever possible, empower him to make decisions for himself. If you are able to do this consistently, most of the time you'll find your child more cooperative when you can't give in or let him decide. If you are attending a wedding and he must put on those uncomfortable shoes, there is no compromise. With some sense of fair play, he may just give into the demand with little fuss. By giving him choices and

letting him make decisions, you are also teaching him to become more independent and think for himself. Ultimately, this is what we want for our children. Powering him into submission will never teach this and is likely to backfire as he becomes more obstinate over time.

Let him save face.
If it's cold and he refuses to wear a jacket, give him options so he'll have it, rather than trying to force it on him or letting him go cold just to prove your point. Don't turn things into a power struggle in which you're right and he's wrong. You don't want him to walk around in wet shoes all day, but if he refuses to wear his boots, you could try giving him the option of taking an extra pair of shoes and socks in his back pack, "just in case." Making decisions we don't agree with is part of his growth process; make this easy on yourself.

Play to his problem-solving ability.
Children with ADD/ADHD enjoy puzzling through things; they have an innate problem-solving ability. Present tasks to be completed as if they are problems to be solved. If you have to clean up the kitchen before you can go to the park, for instance, you might tell him that it will take you two hours to do all of the things you have to do. However, if more than one person were to be doing it, how long does he think it would take? Then, you could offer to work together with him and see if he's right. "How long do you think it would take us to empty the dishwasher? Let's try it and see." This can also work in other ways. You could make the task a game; games are really elaborate problem-solving vehicles. As with any game, there are rules of play that must be followed. If you want him to clean his room you might

tell him he can do anything he wants but he has to stay in his room for 15 minutes and then he has to go play for 15 minutes. Those are the rules of the game and you both have to follow those rules. He can choose to do whatever he wants in his room, but he has to be there as long as the room still needs cleaning. When those 15 minutes is over, he has to play; he can't be in there anymore. When playtime is up, it's up, no matter what he's doing, and he must return to his room for 15 minutes. Once he learns the rules of the game, he will learn to live within them, as long as you are consistent. If he wants to be outside, he will pick up the room as fast as he can in those 15 minutes so that he can go do something else. Change the game, and the rules, to meet your needs and what you need your child to complete.

Listen and try to see his point of view.
You may learn something you didn't know and have the opportunity to teach or to dispel a myth or flaw in his thinking. If a bath is a pain for you, but he refuses to take a shower, find out why. He might have a really good reason. Maybe he's afraid he'll go down the drain or get his foot stuck in it? Maybe he stopped eating raisins because someone at school told him they were dried up pieces of worm. You won't know that if you don't ask and listen for the answer. Maintaining a dialogue with your children at an early age will bond you together, as well. You can't be an advocate for him if you don't know what's going on in his life. Remember that he really wants to please you; he also wants his own sense of control and respect for who he is. If he's angry, does he have a right to be? If you were wrong, admit it and apologize. Treat your children the same way in which you expect to be treated.

Recognize success.

Try to catch your children being good whenever possible and praise them, telling them exactly what behavior you're proud of. Not only does this create a positive relationship between you, but it teaches them how you want them to behave. When you must reprimand, start it with a positive comment: "I love that you want to help me clean the windows, but I don't want you standing on the back of the furniture or it will get wrecked." "I love that you wanted to help, but please don't take hot things out of the microwave because it might burn you." When you really must discipline, make it as emotionless as possible and don't fight with him. If, for example, you tell him to pick up his toys and he doesn't, begin to pick them up and take them, telling him that he will get them back after doing a specific task to re-earn the privilege of having the toy. Don't negotiate and don't fight; remain emotionless. It is what is.

Reward early, reward often, and keep it positive.

Make the rewards fit the goal. It is very hard to keep your eye on a goal if what you're doing is not tied to it in any way. What do stars on a chart really mean? By themselves, they may mean nothing. If, however, the sticker on the chart is one your child gets to choose and put on the chart 'for brushing my teeth,' it will have more meaning to him. You could use a mason jar (which has lines of measure on it) and have him fill it up with marbles or small toys while working toward a bigger reward, such as an outdoor toy. An acrylic tube with a rubber ball could be filled slowly with a measured amount of water for each reward. As your child progresses toward the goal, the ball rises in the tube. You will probably have to change reward measures, and rewards, often because the kids will tire of one and it then becomes less effective.

ADD/ADHD children also tend to have shorter memories. Instead of saying "Brush your teeth, put on your pajamas, put out clothes for the morning," have him brush his teeth, then earn the reward, put on his pajamas and earn another reward, put his clothes out and earn the third reward. Each positive action is a positive step toward his overall goal of pizza, picking the vegetable for dinner, an extra 15 minutes of play at the park, or whatever other mutual reward you set for a larger goal.

Remember to keep it positive. Negative behavior does not negate previous positive behaviors; therefore rewards must not be removed as punishment for failure to meet an expectation.

Make things easy on yourself.
Figure out your child's triggers and eliminate them as much as possible. If you know a situation will be chaotic and over-stimulating, try to avoid it. If your child has trouble sitting at the table and eating, try to provide finger foods that allow him the freedom to move around. Instead of a toy box, use tackle boxes and small containers to organize and store toys. With a toy box, everything comes out in the search of one toy. With a distractible mind, there are so many distractions to choose from on the way down to that toy so, everything comes out; nothing goes back in. Organizing the toys on shelves makes this a little less likely.

Avoid idle time as much as possible without having so many activities that you become stressed and your child becomes over-stimulated. Idle time is merely time to look for trouble. Decrease stimulation at night.

Set some systems in place for you. Disciplinary systems are really in place to help you maintain your cool while setting limits. For Sean, we used a derivative of Thomas W. Phelan's 1-2-3 Magic. This is an entire system, which won't be repeated here. At one point, however, the system allows you to interrupt a behavior by simply saying "That's one-That's two-That's three-Take five." This is a consistent way to give your child three chances to stop before getting a five minute time out. However, as we've already discussed, Sean wouldn't take time out, at all. So, we had to come up with an appropriate and consistent consequence for getting to three. I honestly don't remember what that consequence was now. After less than a handful of times, Sean rarely got past two and usually didn't need more than one. The idea is to call attention to the behavior and give them an opportunity to stop of their own accord. Again, using this technique and being consistent about the consequence is for your benefit more than your child's. It short circuits the power struggle and takes emotion out of the equation.

Another technique you can use is CARE.
- C~Clear away distractions and things that cause inappropriate behaviors.
- A~Allow your child to choose an appropriate activity.
- R~Redirect him into another activity if he grows bored with his choice or becomes disruptive.

- E~Escape. Recognize that the situation is beyond your control, it is about to escalate and there is nothing to be gained by fighting it. Take the children to the park, play in the yard with them or just give in to spending play time with them instead.

CARE is a very good technique to keep in mind when you have things to do, such as getting supper ready. Create a calm environment, get the children involved in an activity of their choosing, redirect them when they start acting up, recognize when it's time to give up and escape.

Set rewards, and consequences that you can live with. Don't take away TV for a week if it means that no one can watch TV or that you will have to fight with the child to keep them from watching. Don't agree to a reward that you will struggle to afford or to take him to the chaotic indoor playground if you can't stand the place for more than 15 minutes.

Have a Special Time.
Spend one-on-one time with each of your children every week. This is an excellent opportunity for the children to express themselves and their concerns. Don't push this as a talk time, however. It's not for therapy or teaching; it's for bonding. You could use this time to go to the park, mall, or for a favorite spot or activity. This time could also be used to play a board game, for story time, or for a child-specific hobby such as arts and crafts, music, or playing a video game together. Getting to know your children and appreciating the amazing person that they are shows a great deal of respect and

will help you remain an advocate for them during rough times.

Take care of you.
Make sure you have plenty of sleep, that you get time to yourself, and that you take time to do things that make you happy. If you are constantly stressed, no amount of positive thinking is going to make things go well when your children just won't seem to listen.

Schools

Schools represent one of the biggest challenges to the families of the ADD-gifted. The rigid standards, large class sizes, clique-filled peer groups, and distraction-ridden environment all work together in a perfect stress storm for the child with ADD.

Like the Special Forces-trained, the ADD-gifted are hyper-aware of their environments. The only difference is environment. Someone in the Special Forces is trained to notice the guy wearing dress shoes at the beach, the dog catcher who isn't chasing the loose dog and has handcuffs in his back pocket, the woman with the baby buggy who never checks the baby. The ADD-gifted hears the teacher, the squeak of the wheels of the milk cart as it comes down the hall, the kids passing a note to his left, the papers on the wall to the right blowing in the breeze from the window or heat vent. If the walls are thin, he hears things from the classroom next door. If he can see out the window, he might watch the birds fly by, or the kids on the playground who have recess while he doesn't. If he's bored, he may even get lost in his own thoughts or start reading during class. Everything is noticed, but nothing takes priority. Not unlike the hyper-awareness of someone on high alert, a chaotic environment can quickly build up the fight-or-flight adrenaline response in the student with ADD. This sometimes causes outbursts, speaking out in class, and even anger responses.

Gifted With ADD © 2011 RaeLyn Murphy

Adding insult to injury, children clan together and can be very cruel to anyone who is "different" in any way. Instead of treating the learning-enabled as an asset, schools tend to view it as a disability and the ADD-gifted are treated as somewhat dysfunctional. Your child is not at all learning-disabled; he is rigid-thinking intolerant. He is not able to sit still, face forward, and pay attention, but he is quite capable of grasping complex concepts much quicker than the majority of the class. And yet, the system of the average public school completely masks this ability.

Take into consideration the first signs that your son or daughter had ADD. He was into everything, wanted to know everything all at once, and probably liked to take things apart to see how they worked. The ADD are hyper-sensory. They learn with all five senses. Learning for them is completely interactive. They are naturally curious. Learning is an engaging, whole-body experience.

Now look at the average school environment. Students sit in hard desks for hours at a time. They must ask permission, and may be denied permission, to go the restroom or get a drink of water. They have recess at assigned times. They are issued standardized tests during which they must be completely silent. When they are to participate in class, most often they have to raise their hand and wait to be called upon. A clock is on the wall in front of them or off to the side in which they can watch the time slowly tick by. The teacher talks *at* the students, inviting participation more for feedback than for engaging discussion, (which would be evidenced by the ability to discuss and not merely answer a question once called upon). Things are written on the board, notes are taken, and penmanship is practiced.

Learning in this environment is passive. The information is given by the teacher, received by the student, and regurgitated in the form of test answers and homework assignments. Homework causes resentment in students and parents alike. After spending six hours in school, the last thing a child wants to do in the evening is more school work. After working all day, the last thing parents want to do is help with school work they have to re-learn in order to help with in the first place. Also, the best after school activity for an ADD-gifted child is activity--sports, Scouts, clubs, martial arts, or just plain playground time. So, parents get to work all day, come home, make supper, taxi their children to activities, and harangue their children into doing their homework all before they get time to relax themselves. The school year, whether your child has ADD or not, is a grind. Personally, I never understood why parents loved it when their kids went back to school.

One final note: have you ever noticed how much attention a whisper draws? If you really want someone to hear what you are saying, whisper it to them. They must lean in and focus completely on what you are saying. Now imagine a quiet room the ADD-gifted way, keeping in mind their hypersensitivity to their surroundings. A silent room is never silent, especially when it is filled with people. There are children kicking the rungs of their desk, someone coughs, the second hand ticks on the clock, pencils scratch the surface of paper, papers are moved around. Tests are taken in quiet rooms to aid in the ability to focus and to reduce the chances of cheating. For the ADD-gifted, this environment is more rife with distractions than a loud, chaotic environment is. This is also good to keep in mind when it comes time for your child to do homework. If they learn better with music, let them have their music.

Public School Success

First, let go of the idea of grades as a benchmark for your child's success. If you have an ADD-gifted child, he's a quick and smart learner. You don't need to fear that he will grow up "stupid." Granted, we don't want our kids to flunk a grade or to end up in the classes for learning disabled. Just don't look to the letter grade as the ultimate gauge of success or failure. As a reward, a letter on a piece of paper once every three months is much too ethereal for, well *most*, children to work toward, anyway. Work with the teacher for more immediate rewards and more continual course correction.

And, by the way, could there be a worse title for a classroom than LD (Learning Disabled)? At a school, children are there to learn. What is with putting them in a classroom which, by very definition, calls them a failure at what they are there to do? I don't care who your child is, putting him in a classroom that is actually labeled "disabled" is inhumane if only for what he must endure on the playground and bus because of it. In the case of the ADD-gifted, however, it's a slap in the face. As the parent, you're being told that the best place for your bright, intelligent, quick-thinking child is the classroom the other students call the "dumb room" because he doesn't learn the same way as the other children. He's not unable to learn and, yes, the smaller class size and reduced distractions, will aid his ability to focus. Wouldn't he be better served in a small classroom for fast learners? Instead of being frowned on for being bored in class and noticing everything, he could learn at his own pace and keep the respect of his peer group.

Now consider this: schools receive extra funding for children with IEP's (Individualized Education Plans) and 504's. While this money is necessary to provide services to students with problems, schools still have a vested interest in taking students out of the regular population and putting them on a plan rather than working with the parents and student for the best interest of the child. If you do opt into the LD program, please make sure your child is getting the services that government funding is paying for.

The Teacher Is NOT The Enemy
Be proactive in your child's education. If you already have a diagnosis, sit down with the teacher and other caregivers. Discuss what works for you and what doesn't. If you use a system of rewards and/or consequences that is very effective, share it with the teacher for consistency between home and school. Discuss expectations and previous successes your child has had with other instructors. Keep in mind that no one knows your child better than you do and remember that you are his advocate. It is your job to run interference for him. If you are meeting opposition from the school, how much more difficult do you think things would be for him without you on his side?

Gifted With ADD © 2011 RaeLyn Murphy

Work out some strategies with the teacher that take care of the "symptoms" or "problems" of ADD/ADHD:

- **Have him sit in a middle seat in the front of the class.**
    - Reduces distractions from the door, hallway, rooms to either side, student disruptions, and things on the walls
    - Allows the teacher the opportunity to provide verbal and visual cues such as tapping on the desk to refocus the student or verbally pointing out "This is important" to signal the child to pay attention to a certain point
    - This grants the teacher more immediate access for real time rewards for good behavior. Often, the best reward is acknowledgement. With the student in the front, a pat on the shoulder, smile, eye contact and "attaboy" are easier to apply and more subtle to the remainder of the class.
    - If you notice the student is grasping things quickly and is, perhaps, getting bored, have him assist a student who doesn't understand it yet. Using his quick-smart ability to the advantage of other students empowers the ADD-gifted and reinforces that he is _able_, not disabled.

- **Alternate seated activities with ones that require movement.**
    - As a bonus, this works well for the whole class and will keep students more engaged.
    - Besides aiding the child's inherent need to move around, incorporating movement in the lesson my access the child's natural full-sensory learning style.
- **Write important things down where he kind find it and access it later.**
    - It may be extra work for the teacher to make sure your child has all of the important notes. Even so, important points will be digested if they are in constant sight or if your child knows where to find them when needed.
    - Empower the student by making sure he looks for the answers instead of giving him the answers when they are readily available to him in other places.
    - Teach students to use a highlighter. If his penmanship is the worst, which is often the case in the ADD-gifted, handing out notes and cueing students in to important points can help them stay focused and find important information later.
- **Allow more frequent breaks.**
    - If you notice the student is getting fidgety, have him run an errand for you such as passing out papers, sharpening pencils,

handing out milk, or grabbing a book off of the shelf from across the room. This positive and proactive step allows the child some freedom of movement and maintains his sense of well-being. It short-circuits the adult "habit" of reacting to negative behavior, instead.
  - A child with ADD may require more bathroom and water breaks. Allowing this, again, provides for his need to move without being obvious.

- **Divide assignments up into smaller chunks for students who can't follow a stream of items as well as others do.**

- **Provide a stress ball or small toy for the student to fidget with discreetly during class.**
  - The simple act of squeezing the ball or doing something quietly with his hands can help to keep the mind focused on the task at hand.

- **Provide time for unrestricted movement outside of class.**
  - Make sure a child with ADD/ADHD never misses Phy Ed or recess.
  - Allow time to run around before and after school.
  - If necessary, allow for a place in the yard or gym in which he can burn off steam during the day before returning to the classroom.

- Help the parents choose an appropriate sport for the ADD-gifted child to participate in.

Pick your battles and give him a break now and then.

- If the child is doing their work and mostly paying attention in class, does it really matter how he's sitting in his desk?
- Allow for the fact that the ADD-gifted student tends to be disorganized. He doesn't mean to forget his homework or turn it in late. Allow him to make it up. If you must give him an F, remember that it's a 65, not a zero. A zero is almost impossible to recover from and it's not right to punish the student for something he can't help.
- Because of disorganization, some students carry their entire locker with them all day in a backpack. Make adjustments for this or help him find a better organizational plan.
- Allow a second set of books at home, in case he forgets a book and to keep the parents in the loop regarding progress.
- If he consistently gets behind or forgets to turn in homework, call home as a courtesy. Take the child out of the loop and don't make phone calls home a "you're in trouble" thing.
- Remember that behavior that is rewarded is usually repeated while behavior that is unacceptable, if ignored, will generally

decrease or disappear. Make it a point to reward early, reward often, and keep things positive.

Tips For School Success At Home
- Establish a folder for finished homework to go in.
- Help your child to make and use checklists. Teach him to scratch through an item once or highlight completed items so that they can still be read in case he needs to refer back to them.
- Work with your child to establish a coding system such as color-coding or themes/decorations on certain folders and files. Math goes in red, English in yellow, Science in blue, etc.
- Get in the habit of checking and organizing the backpack every night alongside your child. Empower through teaching and helping, not correcting.
- Set up a system of study/move/study/move on a 15 minute timer. It should take him less and less time to get into study mode if he knows he's going to have to keep doing that until homework is complete. It will also build in distraction time at regular intervals.
- Have a regular homework place free of distractions, such as TV.
- Find out what works better for your child. Even with ADD, not all noise is disrupting. He may need complete silence, but music can also help one focus the mind at times. During the school day, I thrived in the quiet of the library and grew to love public libraries, as well. But, when I have to get something done and stay focused, I listen

to Techno. Sean listens to Alternative Rock when he needs to focus. Find out what works best for your child. Music is also a fantastic coping mechanism when the day becomes stressful.

Alternatives to School

In 1964, John Holt, a pioneer of home-schooling and unschooling wrote the book, *Learning All The Time*. In it, he describes a child's natural love of learning and their innate curiosity about the world around them. A former educator himself, he noted that schools take away this love of learning and replace it with dread. John Taylor Gatto, a New York City teacher for over 30 years, warns us that schools are *Dumbing Us Down*. He points out that schools program our children rather than teaching them to really think. In *The Teenage Liberation Handbook*, Grace Llewellyn, another former teacher, shows teens how to quit high school and take control of their education and, yes, still attend college. The one thing these three free-thinking authors have in common is a desire to foster learning by encouraging children to think for themselves, find solutions, and explore their world. All three point out that the grind of the public school system does not produce happy, well-adjusted, well-educated adults. Instead, it removes the desire to learn via the very processes it uses to teach. There are alternatives.

Home-Schooling

Usually, there are about three objections, or concerns, about home-schooling. 1) There are horror stories about children who have been home-schooled who were never taught anything and are hopelessly behind. 2) Children who are home-schooled lack the socialization that they naturally get from school. 3) Parents worry that they lack the skill to teach their children at home and that their children will lack a proper education. Let's knock these down one-by-one.

Horror Stories. First of all, if you're reading this book, or even this section of the book, you are probably not a horror story waiting to happen. While there are some true stories out there, the majority of home-schooled children are legitimately home-schooled. People who care enough about their children to want them home all day usually also care enough about their futures to actually desire a future for their child. Also, if you're too lazy to provide any sort of education to your children, chances are that it is easier to put them on a school bus and let someone else take care of them than it is to keep them at home. Overall, the numbers of legitimate home-schooling families far outweigh the number of people who merely keep their children at home.

Another thing to keep in mind is that "hopelessly behind" does not necessarily equal uneducated or "dumb." Home-schoolers do not necessarily follow school schedules, but they are still learning all the time. A home-schooled child who suddenly finds himself in a public school system may appear to be a fish out of water. Nevertheless, he may be light years ahead of his classmates in some subjects. This can be an extremely invisible fact when you consider his ability to spew out book-learning facts as opposed to applying knowledge in real world applications. It is really an apples-to-oranges comparison.

Socialization. Children who are home-schooled have as many, if not more, opportunities to socialize as children who are in school. The quality of that socialization, in fact, tends to be better because they are not subject to daily harassment and judgment. Cub Scouts, Boy Scouts, Girl Scouts, the Boys and Girls Clubs, and sports programs are all available to home-schoolers. Many people are also unaware that the sports teams and events of their local school district are also available to the home-schoolers of that district. Therefore, a home-schooler can take part in the local school district's softball program, for instance, as long as they meet other criteria. Local libraries have calendars of events as do local museums, zoos, and other educational sites in any given town. Many areas offer access to home-school groups which can be an opportunity for home-schooled children to spend time together while also allowing for the discount prices a group receives for field trips. This is also a great way for parents to make friends, get support, and learn from each other. Most local parks and recreation departments offer low-cost classes and even free activities throughout the year. Your church may have a youth program. And, if you live in a neighborhood, your children probably have local friends. Because home-schooling takes away the stress of the school grind (getting up for the bus, school, homework, after school activities, getting ready for the next day's grind, etc) the quality of the time outside of the home is simply more enjoyable.

Lack of Education. As previously discussed, the ADD-gifted are generally blessed with intelligent, rapid fire brains. They are unlikely to grow up "dumb" or even uneducated, just as a baseline. Your ability to teach depends merely on the method you choose and your ability to read, write, and do arithmetic. There are many curricula available should you decide to go about school in a more standardized way. Some local public libraries have entire sections devoted to home-schoolers. There are also curricula and education magazines available at educational supply stores. Depending on your personal skill sets, providing a junior high and high school education may challenge you, but it is likely that you have retained the knowledge base required to teach your child elementary school principles.

Most states will have some requirements of home-schoolers, but home-schooling, itself, is free. To find out what the requirements are in your area, contact your state's Department of Public Instruction or Department of Education. Entire books are written about how to go about teaching your children at home, but many of these books will also contain your state's government information if you can't find it online. You may choose to go with a ready-made curriculum, such as Abeka Books, or you may choose to create your own. As long as you stay within the guidelines, your children will get a well-rounded education. Inspirational stories abound regarding home-schooled children who have gotten into college during their high school years. Indeed, Sean was one of them. While he only attended a tech school, he completed his program at the age of 18, when his former classmates were graduating high school.

One concern that has yet to be addressed is the issue of time and money. Many, if not most, families are two income families. If you are also career-oriented, having a child with ADD may have already put a severe crimp in your lifestyle, but home-schooling may end your career plans altogether. You may be wondering how you will find the time to teach your children at home. You may also be wondering how, if one parent stays home with the children, you are going to make ends meet or afford supplies. Home-schooling an ADD child can become expensive simply because they plow through material at an alarming rate. A second income, however, has its own expenses. To find out if you can afford to quit, look at a calculator, such as the one offered by Kiplinger.com. Alternatively, you can do a web search for "the cost of a second income." Curricula and resources are available online for free. Ultimately, you are the only ones who can decide if home-schooling is within the means of your family's resources. Time-wise, you should be aware that home-schooling generally takes less than five hours per day if you follow the guidelines.

Finally, if you think you cannot spend all day with your children, think again. Home-schooling is a challenge. Children try to get away with as much as possible. Without the stress of the school year, however, you are free to turn off the alarm clocks, stop the morning rush, and see your children for who they really are instead of who an inflexible environment would like to mold them to be. Without the need to sit in a chair and listen for hours at a time, your child may not need medicating which takes constant visits to doctors and school meetings out of the equation. No one need dread the ring of the phone or note home that signals another bad day on the school bus or in the classroom. Your children won't come home wound up or bullied. In short, comparing having the child at home to having a child at school is like comparing apples and oranges. The only similarity is that they're both in the same categorical group.

For more information:
Practical Homeschooling: http://www.practical-homeschooling.org/

IXL: http://www.ixl.com/

Homeschool.com: http://www.homeschool.com/default.asp

Successful Homeschooling.com: http://www.successful-homeschooling.com/free-homeschooling-curriculum.html

Home-Schooling.org: http://www.home-schooling.org/

Teach Your Own: The John Holt Book of Homeschooling by John Holt and Pat Farenga

Unschooling
Unschooling is a laid back version of home-schooling. That is a bit over-simplified, but the premise is that opportunities to learn are all around us and we are learning all of the time. Indeed, as an adult, chances are you can identify a host of things you have learned on your own, without the benefit of a formal education. You learn from the news, from books, the History Channel, cable TV, the Internet, friends, seminars, webinars, conferences, museums, shows, and many

other forums. In reality, it is almost impossible to miss an opportunity to learn at least one new thing every day unless you were actively trying to avoid doing so.

The title, "unschooling," might be a tad deceptive. It is not that these children are avoiding an education; they are simply self-directed. The reason this works especially well with ADD-gifted children is because they are able to focus on subjects that draw and hold their interest. Almost any interest or hobby contains multiple subjects within it. Children who are interested in cooking and baking learn math from measuring and doubling or halving recipes; reading by reading recipes; history and culture if they are interested in the background of Italian food, for instance; science from the interaction of kitchen "chemicals" such as yeast, baking soda, salt, vinegar, eggs and even water in its three forms. Robotics is an electronics science in which children will also learn physics and math. If they must program the robot, they will learn programming, spelling and some English skills. An interest in space science teaches history, English, astronomy, math and possibly some culture. No matter what the interest, a natural learning arc occurs among many disciplines at once.

There remains at least one important caveat to the concept of unschooling and it comes in the form of an analogy. In 1985, Broderbund Software released *Where In The World Is Carmen Sandiego?*, the first in a series of educational video games. The game taught history and geography via a crime mystery in which players had to chase Carmen's minions around the world using clues obtained from the scene of the crime and innocent bystanders, ultimately catching Carmen, herself. The result was an educational TV show and the last truly successful edutainment title. Since then, billions of dollars have been spent in the development of educational software without substantial success. Meanwhile, players everywhere would accidentally learn history, social studies, economics, resource management, and civics from *Civilization* and *Sim City*, games which were originally designed simply to play for fun. Why have these games succeeded so well in an area where intentional edutainment fails? Because they are created for fun. The minute you try to turn something fun into a learning experience, it becomes work. If you try to turn baking into an intentional learning experience, you will lose your audience. If, however, you let your children explore their interests fully, their curiosity will take over and the learning will come naturally.

Do not worry that your child's education will become unbalanced. Consider what you were taught in school and what you remember now. Can you still name the capitol cities of all 50 states? How many historical dates do you remember? Can you name all of the presidents to date in order? If you're not a historian, how does that help you in your daily life? If you took calculus in high school, but don't use it at your job, how much of it do you still remember? If there was a subject you did need for your job, didn't you receive a class, or multiple classes, in that subject in college? As your child learns to develop his passions and interests throughout his life, he will also pick up the knowledge he needs to move forward. You can foster his language skills and ability to read and write through reading. Literature is, by far, the best resource for learning vocabulary. It doesn't have to be in the form of classic novels; any books your child enjoys reading will foster learning. Board games, such as Yahtzee®, Life®, Monopoly®, Scrabble®, and Boggle®, teach early spelling, math and money skills, among other things, in a fun way that makes the learning secondary. Art, in all forms, teach self-expression, spatial analysis, and a multitude of other lessons depending on the discipline. The point is that, by freeing their minds, you are opening up the world of possibilities for them.

For More Information:
Radical Unschooling:
http://www.sandradodd.com/unschooling

Growing Without Schooling:
http://www.holtgws.com/whatisunschoolin.html

Skipping School: http://un-schooled.net/

The Teenage Liberation Handbook by Grace Llewellyn

Learning All The Time by John Holt

Sandra Dodd's Big Book of Unschooling:
http://sandradodd.com/bigbook/

Montessori Schools
The Montessori method is similar to unschooling in that it promotes self-directed learning in the child's natural area of interest. Like unschooling within a family of siblings, it also involves students within a 2-3 year age span of each other. In this way, younger students learn from older students who benefit in their own ways from their roles as mentors. Students work in small groups on similar things. For this reason, class sizes can

occasionally be larger in Montessori schools than in public school classrooms. Students come to depend on each other for help in learning, instead of the teacher alone. It is meant to be an environment which empowers children and fosters their independence. In this way, students develop and "I can" attitude which is facilitated by the adults around them.

While Montessori schools generally don't hand out homework to elementary level students, the school is not without structure or a learning plan. Students must still learn the basic skills. They each have an individualized learning plan and things which they must complete. The main difference is that they have control over how long they'd like to work on something and in what order they would like to complete the items on the plan. They also have a plan that caters directly to their interests while making sure that they learn the basics, too. In this way, classes are not dissimilar to an IEP plan and remedial classes in a public school. However, there is a huge difference in an environment which empowers students versus one which labels them as "disabled."

To an untrained eye, a Montessori classroom may seem chaotic. Students work in small groups on many different things, all at the same time. A child with ADD/ADHD may thrive in an environment of self-directed learning and empowerment. However, depending on the amount of general stimulation in the room, they may also struggle with over-stimulation. There is no "right" fit for every student with every school. For this reason, it is best to visit the school and see if your child and the school seem to be a proper fit.

Gifted With ADD © 2011 RaeLyn Murphy

There are two types of Montessori schools, in general. The Association Montessori Internationale (AMI) maintains the purity of the core philosophies and structures developed by Maria Montessori, the founder of the Montessori Method. The American Montessori Society (AMS) was founded in 1960 by Nancy McCormick Rambusch, an AMI-trained teacher. The AMS utilizes the foundations of the AMI while bringing in aspects of American culture such as world events and technology. Once again, whether or not your child attends an AMS school or an AMI school will depend on which seems right for your family and, most likely, proximity to your home.

For More Information:
Montessori Foundation: http://www.montessori.org/

Modern Montessori International Group: http://www.modernmontessori-intl.com/

USA Montessori: http://www.usamontessori.org/

Association Montessori Internationale: http://www.montessori-ami.org/

American Montessori Society: http://www.amshq.org/

Democratic/Sudbury Schools
Sudbury schools are learning communities, more or less. They are based on the model that there are many ways to learn and that all students share an equal responsibility in their community and for their education. The democratic school philosophy is that learning is something that people do, not something that is done to

them. In other words, students play an active role in their education rather than sitting in a classroom so that someone can fill their brain with information through lectures and homework.

Sudbury schools allow free, unstructured, activities in which teachers are considered advisers more than they are considered instructors. Like unschooling, democratic schools allow students to choose what they will learn, but the school provides students with resources that might be outside of the financial realm for an unschooling family. Sudbury schools allow students to learn from other students and choose what they will work on each day, but unlike Montessori schools, there are no structured class groups or individual lesson plans.

Democratic schools make use of a democratic society within the school. Policies, hiring, firing, and school decisions are all made during whole school meetings in which every student and staff member has an equal vote and an equal voice. Rule infractions are enforced via a judicial committee which is made up of students from the school. While an unstructured environment of kids just "hanging out" for five hours may sound like anti-education, an environment in which students are able to stumble upon new interests simply by being exposed to many people with a variety of interests is what makes this environment work. Students are treated with respect as thinking, feeling, people rather than age groups. In this way, an eleven year old may pick up an interest in algebra from a sixteen year old and an elementary student may inspire a teen to love Shakespeare.

For More Information:
Education Futures:
http://www.educationfutures.org/Respect.htm
New American Schoolhouse:
http://www.newamericanschoolhouse.com/

Did You Learn Anything:
http://www.didyoulearnanything.net/about/sudbury/

Lists of Sudbury Schools in the US:
http://www.educationrevolution.org/lisofdemscho.html#U.S.A.

http://en.wikipedia.org/wiki/List_of_Sudbury_schools#United_States

Waldorf Education

Waldorf education is a more structured school environment which strives to impact the child through lessons that integrate the hands, heart, and head. Age groups define learning style such that children seven and under are believed to be beings of will and movement; children ages seven to fourteen learn through feeling, artistic creation, and imagination; and children fourteen and up experience the world in more logical, analytical, and conceptual ways. Teachers follow students through the grades, giving students a greater opportunity to be known and understood by their teacher as they grow. This helps the teacher get to know learning styles and aid the process as each child progresses through the educational phases.

The founder, Rudolf Steiner, found that children learn better when the lesson awakens the mind, touches the heart, and engages the hands. For this reason, art and music are integrated into most lessons. This is viewed as a more holistic approach to education. Despite the more structured school environment, a Waldorf education may speak to the more creative learning style of the ADD-gifted child.

For more information:
Association of Waldorf Schools of North America:
http://www.whywaldorfworks.org/

Waldorf Education Links:
http://www.waldorfanswers.org/WaldorfLinks.html

Lists of US schools:
http://members.awsna.org/Public/SchoolListPage.aspx

http://www.educationrevolution.org/lisofdemscho.html#U.S.A.

Video Links:
http://www.youtube.com/results?search_query=waldorf+school&aq=0&oq=Waldorf+school

Coalition of Essential Schools
Essential schools feature project-based lessons. Founded in 1984 by Theodore Sizer, Essential Schools are still very young, but the movement has been growing steadily. Sizer, a former dean of Harvard's School of Education, had done a study of American schools and found that the existing system lacked a proper sense of motivation for students. Instead, students took part in a standardized education, took

standardized tests, and many were merely "serving time" until graduation.

Project-based learning takes a more holistic, "multiple intelligence" type approach. Students learn in many ways; only a small portion are audio-visual learners--the type who learn from being lectured. Standard schools tend to cater only to this type of student, leaving kinesthetic learners--those that need to experience things for themselves in order to absorb the lesson--to struggle. With project-based learning, students absorb the entire lesson using a variety of methods.

There are ten principles on which the Coalition of Essential Schools is founded:

1. **Learning to use one's mind well**--Learning is something that people do, not something which is done to them. Therefore, it should be the goal of the school to help students find information for themselves.
2. **Less is more, depth over coverage**--The goal of the school should be student mastery of the content they are learning, not the quantity of material that can be taught and reproduced for tests.
3. **Goals apply to all students**--The school's goals should apply to all students, but how the students reach those goals will be as varied as the students, themselves. School policies should be tailor-made to meet the needs of every group or class of students.
4. **Personalization**--Teaching and learning should be personalized as much as possible. To accomplish this, smaller class sizes are

necessary to allow for individual needs. For this reason, decisions about the school policies, books, means and practices should remain in the hands of the staff of the school rather than being state or federally mandated.

5. **Student-as-worker, teacher-as-coach**--The main focus of an Essential School should remain on the student's learning and, therefore, on the student's ability to teach himself. Teachers provide focus and guidance in a coaching position instead of serving as the authority on the subject.

6. **Demonstration of mastery**--It is important to assess the competence of students and mastery of subject matter using a variety of tools. If a student is not yet showing mastery, intensive support and resources should be provided to help them meet the appropriate standards quickly. In this way, assessment is not a matter of judgment in which a student passes or fails. Instead, it is a measure of understanding from which coaches can develop a plan to help the student get where he needs to be. A diploma is awarded once students demonstrate final mastery of the subject as demonstrated through exhibitions. Since the diploma is thus awarded when earned, there is no strict age requirement nor is there a system of credits earned based on time spent in class.

7. **A tone of decency and trust**--The tone of the school should stress the values of expectation free of threats, of trust, and of proper behavior which includes fairness, generosity and tolerance toward everyone. Incentives appropriate to the school's particular students

and teachers should be emphasized. Parents should be key collaborators and vital members of the school community.
8. **Commitment to the entire school**--The principal and teachers should perceive themselves as generalists first (coaches and leaders) and specialists second (experts in but one particular discipline). Staff should expect to serve in many different roles and have a sense of commitment to the entire school and its students.
9. **Resources dedicated to teaching and learning**--Ultimately, administrative and budgetary goals should include student loads that promote personalization, considerable time for teachers to gather for planning, competitive salaries for staff, and an ultimate per pupil cost not to exceed that at traditional schools by more than 10 percent.
10. **Democracy and equity** The school should demonstrate non-discriminatory and inclusive policies, practices, and lesson plans. It should model democratic practices that involve all who are directly affected by the school. The school should honor diversity and build on the strength of its communities.

For More Information:

Coalition of Essential Schools: http://en.wikipedia.org/wiki/Coalition_of_Essential_Schools

Essential Schools: http://www.essentialschools.org/

Coalition Center for Essential School Reform:
http://www.antiochne.edu/acsr/ces/

College Instead of High School
There are actually many ways in which a student may attend college courses or learn a vocation while still in high school. Some of these, such as an apprenticeship program or actually skipping high school to attend college, will not result in a high school diploma, so the student would need to obtain a High School Equivalency Diploma (HSED). Others, however, allow the student to attain college credits and high school credits simultaneously.

While it may be possible to find programs that are available to younger students, the majority of these college-level programs require the student to be at least 16 years of age and "in good standing" in their high school program. This is largely because there will be no hand-holding. In a college setting, the high school student does not stand out, nor are they treated differently from other students attending classes there. Acceptance into the program is also not a "given."

Program details will vary by program and school district. In some areas, the college classes are offered directly in district high schools. In others, the students are required to transport themselves to the college. Programs, such as Wisconsin's Youth Options program, pay for college classes as long as the high school doesn't offer a program which they feel is equivalent. While a high school auto shop class offers no significant comparison to a tech school Auto Technician program, the school may refuse to pay for the Auto Tech classes based on this rule. This does not exclude the student from attending the college classes--high school auto shop does not offer any college credits, after all. It frees the school from the obligation to pay for the class, something which is normally a benefit of attending these programs for the student. College Instead of High School students are normally ineligible for federal college grant programs. Therefore, if the high school does not pay for "competing classes," the money will have to come from the student's family. The program, however, is of obvious overall benefit to students who are able to attend. Provided that the student will obtain enough credits to graduate high school and has the maturity necessary to handle their own college career, students graduate high school with college credits, and possibly, with an Associate's Degree.

Students as young as 16, in good standing at school, may be eligible for apprenticeship programs or the Job Corps. Apprenticeships grant students the opportunity to learn a vocation, hands on. These programs change regularly, but may include anything from construction work to office jobs. Contact your local Office of Apprenticeship for programs in your area. In similar fashion, the Job Corps matches eligible students with participating companies which train them for a job with the option of later hiring them, as well.

Students "in good standing" may be eligible to attend college as a full time college student. It may seem counter-intuitive but, if your child is struggling in high school, it may be in his best interest to home school for a year. This takes "good standing" out of the equation and allows them to enter college, with financial aid, provided that they can pass the entrance exams and meet entrance requirements. Financial Aid does get a bit tricky for underage students, however. Male students are required to register with Selective Service, for instance. Unregistered males are ineligible for some forms of financial aid until they comply, but males under 18 may not register. This does not mean, however, that your son would be ineligible for financial aid until he is 18; alert the college financial aid office of the issue ahead of time to receive assistance in this area.

For More Information:
Career Focus: http://www.careerfocuscafe.com/career-news/college-instead-high-school.php

Early College High School Initiative:
http://www.earlycolleges.org/overview.html

Apprenticeship Eligibility According To The US Department of Labor:
http://www.doleta.gov/jobseekers/apprent.cfm

State Offices of Apprenticeship:
http://www.doleta.gov/oa/stateoffices.cfm

Department of Labor Youth Programs:
http://www.dol.gov/dol/topic/training/youth.htm

Job Corps: http://www.jobcorps.gov/Home.aspx

'How Are We Going To Pay For That?':

At this point, you may be thinking that alternative schools sound like something you'd like try. If money is a problem, don't give up yet. There may be solutions you are unaware of. Beware: You should never have to pay anyone to find financial aid programs. This includes grant databases with paid subscriptions. This information is readily available for free. Do not pay for it.

Most private schools have some sort of financial aid office. If yours is not immediately apparent, contact the administrative offices. If the school, itself, doesn't offer financial aid services, they may be able to direct you to the proper resources. Since it is in their best interest to have a student population, most schools will be willing to assist parents in finding the funds to afford it.

The Department of Education in your state may also offer vouchers or financial assistance for your state. See the links below to find contact information for your state's Department of Education. Grants may be available, as well. Usually, grants and scholarships are limited to college-level students, but there are foundations that do support private school educations.

Loans may also be available. Some of these links will point you in the direction of loan resources in addition to grants and scholarships. Grants and scholarships are "free money"--if you meet the qualifications for these, you will not have to repay the money. Loans must be repaid and it is not the advice of this author that parents go into debt to pay for the education of their children, so specific loan links are not included.

For More Information:
Financing A Private Education:
http://www.nais.org/about/index.cfm?ItemNumber=145880

Financial Aid Advice for Private School Educations:
http://www.theprivateschooljournal.com/content/view/27/

State Departments of Education:
http://wdcrobcolp01.ed.gov/Programs/EROD/org_list.cfm?category_ID=SEA

National Association of Independent Schools Financial Aid Applications:
http://sss.nais.org/Parents/FinAidResources/content.cfm?ItemNumber=152523&navItemNumber=152524

Children's Scholarship Fund:
http://www.scholarshipfund.org/drupal1/

Black Student Fund:
http://www.blackstudentfund.org/index.aspx

A Better Chance:
http://www.abetterchance.org/abetterchance.aspx?pgID=868

Choice Programs (For Financial Aid) By State:
http://www.edreform.com/School_Choices/Choice_Programs/?Choice_Options_State_by_State

Financial Aid Resource Database: http://www.finaid.org/

Private Scholarship Programs:
http://www.edreform.com/Archive/?Private_Scholarship_Programs_A_Matter_Of_Priorities

Conclusion

This has not, by any means, been a comprehensive look at school options. Charter classes vary, in name and in content, by state and school district. Students may be able to attend local and college classes online. The International Baccalaureate program allows students yet another alternative to high school; options are available via the foreign exchange program, as well.

The one thing the majority of alternative school programs seem to have in common is the desire to take a more holistic approach to education. These programs recognize that there are different learning styles and that learning needs will vary by student base. They also share an ability to flex more along with the developmental cycles of childhood than traditional schools do.

The main thing to keep in mind is that you are attempting to help your child get the best education possible while derailing the stress-filled aspect of trying to get your child to adhere to policies that don't fit his personality or learning style. The goal is to socially acclimate your child, not to mold him into something he can never be. If you are struggling with schools at present, it may seem as if school success and a peaceful home life are out of reach. In this pattern, ADD/ADHD is a disease to be treated and dealt with. When you interrupt the pattern and help your child find a program that speaks to his highest good, he will find success beyond the current imagination of any of you and excel. The ADD-gifted have a tremendous capacity to absorb phenomenal amounts of information and utilize it in ways he would never even have the opportunity to demonstrate in a traditional school. The key is to unlock his ability to do so. Traditional schools will tell you that your child is "disabled" and needs help, but their method of help is to dumb down your child's innate abilities.

Adults With ADD

If you do an Internet search for adult ADD, the results are largely negative. Women speak out about being in failed relationships with an ADD male. There is job difficulty and, once again, the focus rests largely on how one should go about dealing with the fact that they are cursed with this dread disease. Estimates vary regarding what percentage of children with ADD continue to exhibit symptoms into adulthood, but the broad spectrum is somewhere between 30 and 70 percent. As an inherited trait, you don't really outgrow it; you simply learn to live with it.

Adults with ADD may have difficulty at work. Because they are so quick-thinking, they have difficulty respecting people in authority over them. That spontaneous mouth they had as a child isn't always censored as an adult. Boring, repetitive work doesn't serve their needs. Working in an environment in which they have to deal with the general public is stressful, at the very least. Significant others find the ADD-gifted forgetful, easily distractible, irritable, and poor with money.

Part of the problem, however, rests with how we are treating ADD/ADHD in childhood. If children grow up with the message that ADD/ADHD is a debilitating curse in which they do not fit in everyday society and medication is necessary to make them "normal," how will they ever learn deal with who they really are as a person? By helping your child find his strengths and the blessing of his being during childhood, these issues should be non-existent, for the most part. There will still be times when the ADD-gifted adult needs to find himself. Job satisfaction can be hit-or-miss. However, job satisfaction is hit-or-miss for many people. Many people are bad with money.

It was mentioned earlier that the ADD-gifted most likely aren't cut out for factory work or retail jobs. They need stimulation, interesting work, and have no filter for dealing with "stupid people." That's a brutal statement, but unfortunately, that is how they view it. This is not to say that retail employees or factory workers are in any way diminished. These jobs are filled with hard-working, intelligent, college graduates who are doing what is best for their families. Anyone who treats any employee in any job as if they are "less" in some way should be ashamed of themselves.

That aside, the ADD-gifted do excel in jobs that would drive others to their knees. Fast-paced, high-tech, high-stress environments are a dream come true. These environments fuel their love of all things cutting edge, provide constant stimulation, and allow their quick-thinking brains a place to thrive. As a parent who desires to help their child find a future for themselves, the only thing you really need to do is help them find their passions. Growing up, there will be subject matter that the child just can't seem to get enough of. Steer them in this direction and they will navigate into adulthood with relative ease.

Gifted With ADD © 2011 RaeLyn Murphy

If, for some reason, your child doesn't demonstrate a strong interest in one or two subjects, the main things to keep in mind are his need for stimulation, interesting work, and a hands-on environment. College may seem to offer the same challenges as public school: learning through lectures, sitting still in a desk, and a distracting environment. Some classes will, indeed, present these challenges. However, since the student is choosing the school program, if they have chosen an area of interest, most of the subject matter will hold their attention. If it doesn't, it will become clear, rather quickly, that this is the wrong career to pursue. This does present family challenges, especially for a student who "never really stuck with anything" and now finds he needs to tell his parents he's switching majors. Try to understand. Help him, if you can, to find an engrossing career that allows for some hands-on education time in the form of labs, experiments, or shop classes.

Adults with ADD also make great entrepreneurs. In this way, they take a leadership role and also have the ability to engage in the risk-taking behavior so inherent to their personalities. You will recall that Richard Branson, founder of Virgin Airlines and renowned risk-taker, has ADD. Also suspected of ADD were Alexander Graham Bell, Thomas Edison, Albert Einstein, and Frank Lloyd Wright. The point is not that they were or are successful, but the kinds of things they've done to find those successes. Don't let fear hold you back; the ADD-gifted are fearless, which is the secret to their success.

Be Like Water

The first time you hear that your child has ADD, you may feel crestfallen. This surely doesn't sound like a good thing. After all, while there are plenty of success stories regarding people with ADD/ADHD, the diagnosis is rarely the featured part of the story. As a parent, the main story you hear is about medications, doctors, and school difficulties. When it's your child, it feels like a curse.

And yet, you picked up this book, and probably sought that very diagnosis, so that you could move on from there and find the best way to help your child. I can't say this strongly enough: derail the school train. Stop the pattern of thinking that contributes to a negative outlook in its tracks. The majority of the stress in the ADD household comes from trying to bend a willful child to conform to a standard they are simply unable to conform to.

People around you will be telling you that your child lacks discipline. You feel that, too. Stories in the news consistently report a lack of parental control and discipline in today's society. There is a great deal of pressure to make sure your children grow up happy, healthy, polite, and well-adjusted and parents will pull their hair out trying to make that happen. In the process, you end up fighting your own nature and the nature of your child to meet societal standards. Stop.

When life becomes a constant daily battle, tempers rise and solutions are not easy to find. Your child becomes increasingly unruly and you, in an attempt to "do the right thing," become a screaming dictator or simply verbally abusive. The more you try to do everything you're told is right, the worse things seem to get. At best, you may find a satisfactory status quo.

Once you stop trying to live up to the demands and expectations of others, however, the tension slips away. Love and acceptance give way to a child who is truly delightful to talk to and spend time with. Be careful; he may teach you something. He'll probably teach you a lot of things. Allow your family to learn and grow together and the harmony will return. Do not worry that your child will grow up uneducated; that is almost impossible. Let it go. Let it all go.

If I could only leave you with one thought, that would be the thought: Don't fight ADD, revel in it. Be like water~let things flow.

Made in the USA
San Bernardino, CA
14 January 2018